COLLEGE COLORING BOOKS

Coloring for Credit

SWEARING WITH SHAKESPEARE

We love seeing completed work! Share your pics with us on social media or send via e-mail to gallery@collegecoloringbooks.com.

Request your custom coloring book today! Colleges, universities, sororities, fraternities, towns, and organizations can now request custom-designed adult coloring books for on- and off-campus bookstores, student/staff activities, admissions/recruiting, community and alumni fundraisers, and more. Special discounts are available on quantity purchases.

College Coloring Books

🌐 www.collegecoloringbooks.com   ✉ info@collegecoloringbooks.com   ☏ +1.571.424.1994

f fb.me/CollegeColoringBooks   🐦 @collegecoloring   📷 @college_coloring_books

ISBN-10: 1-945707-08-9   ISBN-13: 978-1-945707-08-7

Made in the USA

Thou art the rudest welcome to this world

Pericles

Thy sin's not accidental, but a trade

Measure for Measure

Draw thy tool.
My naked
weapon is out.

Romeo and Juliet

Much Ado About Nothing

Thou art a flesh monger, a fool, and a coward

Measure for Measure

Were I like thee I'd throw away myself

Timon of Athens

THOU CREAM FACED FACED LOON

Macbeth

Your virginity breeds mites, much like a cheese

All's Well That Ends Well

Thy tongue outvenoms all the worms of Nile

Cymbeline

Richard III

I'll pray a THOUSAND PRAYERS for thy death

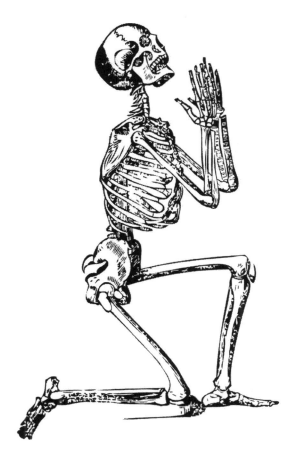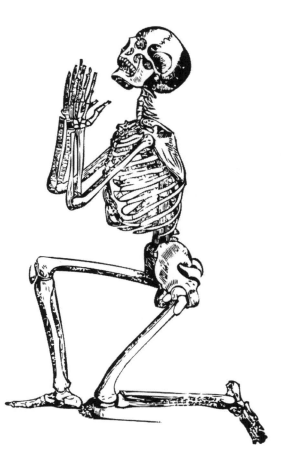

Measure for Measure

thou art a disease that must be

cut away

Coriolanus

Drop into
the rotten
mouth of
death

Richard III

The Taming of the Shrew

King Lear

THOU ART BASER THAN A CUTPURSE

The Two Noble Kinsmen

YOU SCULLION
YOU RAMPALLIAN
YOU FUSTILARIAN
I'LL TICKLE YOUR
CATASTROPHE

Henry IV, Part Two

Take you me for a sponge?

Hamlet

You vile standing tuck

Henry IV, Part One

DEGENERATE AND BASE AND ART THOU

The Two Gentlemen of Verona

The most infectious pestilence upon thee!

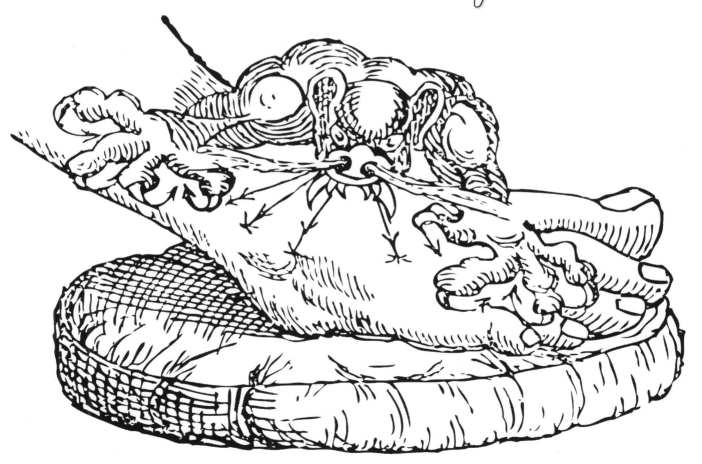

Antony and Cleopatra

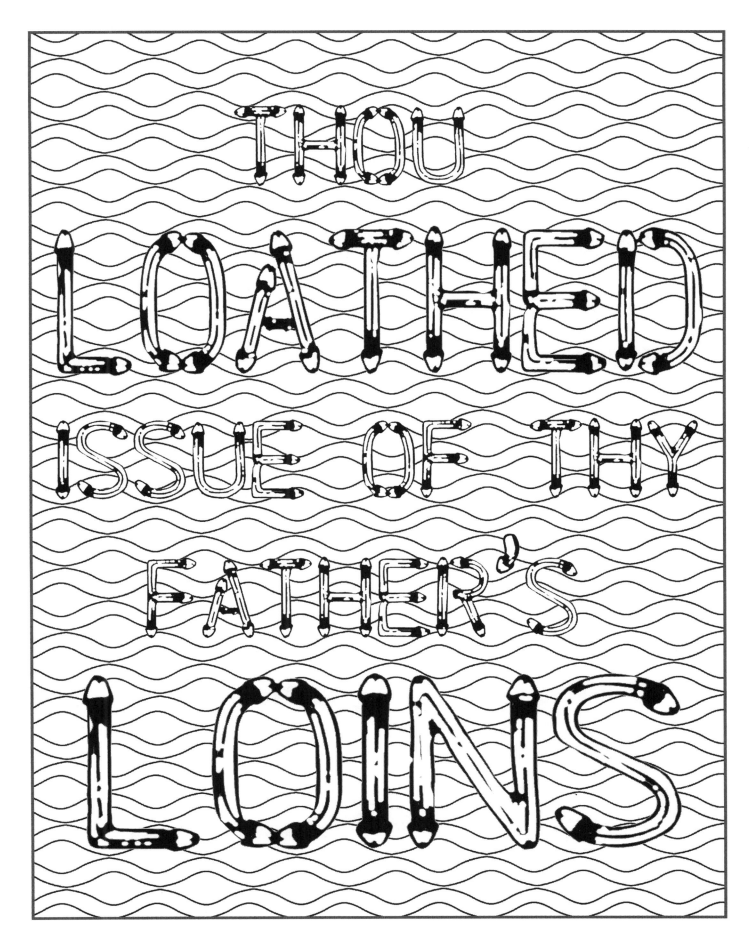

Richard III

THOU DOST INFECT MY EYES

Richard III

The Two Gentlemen of Verona

Thou SMELL of mountain GOAT

BAAAA

Henry V

You shall stifle in your own report, and smell of calummy

Measure for Measure

Troilus and Cressida

Sweep on, you fat and greasy citizens

As You Like It

99124598R00035

Made in the USA
Lexington, KY
13 September 2018